What happens when
Fire
Burns?

Daphne Butler

SIMON & SCHUSTER
YOUNG BOOKS

This book was conceived for
Simon & Schuster Young Books by
Globe Enterprises of Nantwich, Cheshire

Design: SPL Design
Photographs: ZEFA

First published in Great Britain in 1993
by Simon & Schuster Young Books
Campus 400, Maylands Avenue
Hemel Hempstead, Herts HP2 7EZ

Printed and bound in Singapore
by Kim Hup Lee Printing Co Pte Ltd

A catalogue record for this book is available
from the British Library
ISBN 0 7500 1295 1

Contents

Flickering flames

It's very comforting to sit by a warm fire on a cold evening. Flames flicker and dance making friendly shadows around the room.

How do you keep warm on a cold night? Do you sit by a fire?

In a safe place

Fires can be dangerous so they are always made in a fireplace. The smoke escapes to the outside through a chimney.

A fire-guard, fixed around the fireplace keeps people safe from the fire.

Cooking by fire

Some people cook their food over a fire.

Others cook theirs over burning gas.

How does your family cook food?

Lighting a fire

Fires don't happen on their own.
Something must start them.

Gas fires are usually started
by pressing a button that lights
the gas. How might you light a
coal fire?

Never light a fire yourself.
Always ask and adult to help.
If you have an accident you
could be badly burnt.

Sometimes a fire starts by accident. Suddenly, the whole building is on fire.

What sort of things could cause an accident like this?

A smoke alarm would warn if a fire was starting.

Fighting fires

If there is a fire, the fire-brigade will rush along with a fire-engine.

They spray water on to the fire to quench the flames.

The water often comes from the water-main in the street.

17

Fire is always a danger if lorries or planes crash. Their fuel catches light easily and burns fiercely.

Firemen wear fireproof clothing.
They spray foam to smother the
fire. If they use water the burning
fuel will float on top.

Fire in the countryside

The countryside becomes very dry in a long, hot summer.

Fires start easily and are difficult to stop. The wind carries the fire along.

Gaps in the trees called fire-breaks can halt the fire, so can rivers.

What other things would put out the fire?

Explosions

Gas is carried to our homes by pipes under the streets. If the pipes leak and no one notices, the gas could explode.

Petrol stations have huge tanks of fuel under the ground.

What might happen in an earthquake?

Air pollution

Power stations burn coal, oil or gas to make electricity. Cars, lorries and planes burn fuel in their engines.

Dirty gases are given off into the air which becomes unhealthy to breathe. They mix with the rain making acid which kills trees and damages buildings.

When a fire has finally gone out and everything has cooled down, there is an awful mess to clean up.

Countryside is black and charred
after a fire. It will be some time
before plants grow again and trees
will take years to replace.

Fire words

acid rain When exhaust gases mix with the rain they make it acid. The acid falls on trees and kills them. It falls on buildings and eats into the stone.

fire-bricks Bricks made of material that can withstand the heat of a fire without cracking. They are used in fireplaces and furnaces.

28

fire blanket A blanket made of material that does not burn. If put over a small fire, it smothers the flames.

fire extinguisher
A container full of foam that can be sprayed onto a small fire. Useful in a kitchen or in a car.

fireproof clothing
Clothing worn by firemen to protect them from heat and sparks when fighting a fire.

Index